Happy Father's Day

To

Bro. Tom

FROM

Bro Sammy

DATE

June 15, 2008

Promises from God for Father

© 2007 Christian Art Gifts, RSA
 Christian Art Gifts Inc., IL, USA

Designed by Christian Art Gifts
Compiled by Annegreth Botha

Printed in China

ISBN 978-1-86920-757-1

07 08 09 10 11 12 13 14 15 16 – 10 9 8 7 6 5 4 3 2 1

Promises from God for

Father

christian
art gifts®

Contents

ACCEPTANCE

For you are a people holy to the LORD your God. The LORD your God has chosen you out of all the peoples on the face of the earth to be his people, his treasured possession.

Deuteronomy 7:6

Know that the LORD, He is God; it is He who has made us, and not we ourselves; we are His people and the sheep of His pasture.

Psalm 100:3 NKJV

Receive one another, just as Christ also received us, to the glory of God.

Romans 15:7 NKJV

"Those the Father has given me will come to me, and I will never reject them. For I have come down from heaven to do the will of God who sent me."

John 6:37-38 NLT

The LORD appeared to us in the past, saying: "I have loved you with an everlasting love; I have drawn you with loving-kindness."

Jeremiah 31:3

The LORD has heard my cry for mercy; the LORD accepts my prayer.

Psalm 6:9

The Lord disciplines those he loves, and he punishes those he accepts as his children.

Hebrews 12:6 NLT

Now, thus says the LORD, who created you, O Jacob, and He who formed you, O Israel: "Fear not, for I have redeemed you; I have called you by your name; you are Mine."

Isaiah 43:1 NKJV

We are his workmanship, created in Christ Jesus for good works, which God prepared beforehand, that we should walk in them.

Ephesians 2:10 ESV

While we live, we live to please the Lord. And when we die, we go to be with the Lord. So in life and in death, we belong to the Lord. Christ died and rose again for this very purpose, so that he might be Lord of those who are alive and of those who have died.

Romans 14:8-9 NLT

Truly I understand that God shows no partiality, but in every nation anyone who fears him and does what is right is acceptable to him.

Acts 10:34-35 ESV

Jesus said, "I tell you the truth, whoever accepts anyone I send accepts me; and whoever accepts me accepts the one who sent me."

John 13:20

Blessings

But He gives more grace. Therefore He says: "God resists the proud, but gives grace to the humble."

James 4:6 NKJV

Open your mouth and taste, open your eyes and see – how good GOD is. Blessed are you who run to him.

Psalm 34:8 THE MESSAGE

Blessed are those who trust in the LORD and have made the LORD their hope and confidence.

Jeremiah 17:7 NLT

See, I am setting before you today a blessing and a curse – the blessing if you obey the commands of the LORD your God that I am giving you today.

Deuteronomy 11:26-27

The LORD bless you and keep you; the LORD make his face to shine upon you and be gracious to you; the LORD lift up his countenance upon you and give you peace.

Numbers 6:24-26 ESV

Don't repay evil for evil. Don't retaliate when people say unkind things about you. Instead, pay them back with a blessing. That is what God wants you to do, and he will bless you for it.

1 Peter 3:9 NLT

The blessing of the LORD makes one rich, and He adds no sorrow with it.

Proverbs 10:22 NKJV

Blessed is he who has regard for the weak;
the LORD delivers him in times of trouble.

Psalm 41:1

The LORD will give strength to His people;
the LORD will bless His people with peace.

Psalm 29:11 NKJV

Blessed is the man who does not walk in
the counsel of the wicked or stand in the
way of sinners or sit in the seat of mockers.
But his delight is in the law of the LORD, and
on his law he meditates day and night.

Psalm 1:1-2

Bless the LORD, O my soul, and forget not
all his benefits, who forgives all your iniquity, who heals all your diseases.

Psalm 103:2-3 ESV

CHILDREN

Train a child in the way he should go, and when he is old he will not turn from it.

Proverbs 22:6

Whoever believes that Jesus is the Christ is born of God, and everyone who loves Him who begot also loves him who is begotten of Him. By this we know that we love the children of God, when we love God and keep His commandments.

1 John 5:1-2 NKJV

"I will teach your children and make them successful," says the LORD.

Isaiah 54:13 CEV

Children, obey your parents in the Lord, for this is right.

Ephesians 6:1 ESV

The righteous man leads a blameless life; blessed are his children after him.

Proverbs 20:7

Discipline your children, and they will give you happiness and peace of mind.

Proverbs 29:17 NLT

"Believe in the Lord Jesus, and you will be saved, you and your household."

Acts 16:31 ESV

For I will pour water on him who is thirsty, and floods on the dry ground; I will pour My Spirit on your descendants, and My blessing on your offspring.

Isaiah 44:3 NKJV

Children

If you refuse to discipline your children, it proves you don't love them; if you love your children, you will be prompt to discipline them.

Proverbs 13:24 NLT

From everlasting to everlasting the LORD's love is with those who fear him, and his righteousness with their children's children.

Psalm 103:17

Behold, children are a heritage from the LORD, the fruit of the womb a reward. Like arrows in the hand of a warrior are the children of one's youth.

Psalm 127:3-4 ESV

Even a child is known by his actions, by whether his conduct is pure and right.

Proverbs 20:11

Confidence

Being confident of this very thing, that He who has begun a good work in you will complete it until the day of Jesus Christ.

Philippians 1:6 NKJV

Abide in him, so that when he appears we may have confidence and not shrink from him in shame at his coming.

1 John 2:28 ESV

Let us then approach the throne of grace with confidence, so that we may receive mercy and find grace to help us in our time of need.

Hebrews 4:16

Christ Jesus our Lord, in whom we have boldness and access with confidence through faith in Him. Therefore I ask that you do not lose heart at my tribulations for you, which is your glory.

Ephesians 3:11-13 NKJV

The LORD will be your confidence and will keep your foot from being caught.

Proverbs 3:26 ESV

Such confidence as this is ours through Christ before God. Not that we are competent in ourselves to claim anything for ourselves, but our competence comes from God.

2 Corinthians 3:4-5

Now this is the confidence that we have in Him, that if we ask anything according to His will, He hears us. And if we know that He hears us, whatever we ask, we know that we have the petitions that we have asked of Him.

1 John 5:14-15 NKJV

I know that my Redeemer lives, and that he will stand upon the earth at last.

Job 19:25 NLT

That is why I am suffering as I am. Yet I am not ashamed, because I know whom I have believed, and am convinced that he is able to guard what I have entrusted to him for that day.

2 Timothy 1:12

It is the LORD who goes before you. He will be with you; he will not leave you or forsake you. Dot not fear or be dismayed.

Deuteronomy 31:8 ESV

Yea, though I walk through the valley of the shadow of death, I will fear no evil; for You are with me; Your rod and Your staff, they comfort me.

Psalm 23:4 NKJV

COURAGE

Be of good courage, and He shall strengthen your heart, all you who hope in the LORD.

Psalm 31:24 NKJV

He gives strength to the weary and increases the power of the weak.

Isaiah 40:29

For I live in eager expectation and hope that I will never do anything that causes me shame, but that I will always be bold for Christ, as I have been in the past, and that my life will always honor Christ.

Philippians 1:20 NLT

But you, take courage! Do not let your hands be weak, for your work shall be rewarded.

2 Chronicles 15:7 ESV

"Be strong and of good courage, do not fear nor be afraid of them; for the LORD your God, He is the One who goes with you. He will not leave you nor forsake you."

Deuteronomy 31:6 NKJV

Christ is faithful as a son over God's house. And we are his house, if we hold on to our courage and the hope of which we boast.

Hebrews 3:6

In your strength I can crush an army; with my God I can scale any wall.

Psalm 18:29 NLT

"The LORD will fight for you, and you shall hold your peace."

Exodus 14:14 NKJV

"Be strong and courageous. Do not be frightened, and do not be dismayed, for the LORD your God is with you wherever you go."

Joshua 1:9 ESV

Those who hope in the LORD will renew their strength. They will soar on wings like eagles; they will run and not grow weary, they will walk and not be faint.

Isaiah 40:31

"Fear not, for I am with you; be not dismayed, for I am your God; I will strengthen you, I will help you, I will uphold you with my righteous right hand."

Isaiah 41:10 ESV

Do not be afraid of those nations, for the LORD your God is among you, and he is a great and awesome God.

Deuteronomy 7:21 NLT

Discipline

Blessed is the man whom God corrects; so do not despise the discipline of the Almighty.

Job 5:17

Chasten your son while there is hope, and do not set your heart on his destruction.

Proverbs 19:18 NKJV

"My son, do not make light of the Lord's discipline, and do not lose heart when he rebukes you, because the Lord disciplines those he loves, and he punishes everyone he accepts as a son."

Hebrews 12:5-6

Happy are those whom you discipline, Lord.

Psalm 94:12 NLT

Whoever heeds instruction is on the path to life, but he who rejects reproof leads others astray.

Proverbs 10:17 ESV

To learn, you must love discipline; it is stupid to hate correction.

Proverbs 12:1 NLT

No discipline is enjoyable while it is happening – it is painful! But afterward there will be a quiet harvest of right living for those who are trained in this way.

Hebrews 12:11 NLT

Discipline your children; you'll be glad you did – they'll turn out delightful to live with.

Proverbs 29:17 THE MESSAGE

You, fathers, do not provoke your children to wrath, but bring them up in the training and admonition of the Lord.

Ephesians 6:4 NKJV

When we are judged by the Lord, we are being disciplined so that we will not be condemned with the world.

1 Corinthians 11:32

It is better for a man to hear the rebuke of the wise than to hear the song of fools.

Ecclesiastes 7:5 ESV

So you should realize that just as a parent disciplines a child, the LORD your God disciplines you to help you. So obey the commands of the LORD your God by walking in his ways and fearing him.

Deuteronomy 8:5-6 NLT

Encouragement

"Be strong and do not let your hands be weak, for your work shall be rewarded!"

2 Chronicles 15:7 NKJV

Do not gloat over me, my enemy! Though I have fallen, I will rise. Though I sit in darkness, the LORD will be my light.

Micah 7:8

He tends his flock like a shepherd: He gathers the lambs in his arms and carries them close to his heart; he gently leads those that have young.

Isaiah 40:11

Delight yourself in the LORD, and he will give you the desires of your heart.

Psalm 37:4 ESV

For I can do everything with the help of Christ who gives me the strength I need.

Philippians 4:13 NLT

If we are faithful to the end, trusting God just as firmly as when we first believed, we will share in all that belongs to Christ.

Hebrews 3:14 NLT

The LORD is good to those who wait for Him, to the soul who seeks Him. It is good that one should hope and wait quietly for the salvation of the LORD.

Lamentations 3:25-26 NKJV

God equipped me with strength and made my way blameless. He made my feet like the feet of a deer and set me secure on the heights.

Psalm 18:32-33 ESV

"Do not let your heart faint, do not be afraid, and do not tremble or be terrified because of them; for the Lord your God is He who goes with you, to fight for you against your enemies, to save you."

Deuteronomy 20:3-4 NKJV

May our Lord Jesus Christ and God our Father, who loved us and in his special favor gave us everlasting comfort and good hope, comfort your hearts and give you strength in every good thing you do and say.

2 Thessalonians 2:16-17 NLT

Let us not give up meeting together, as some are in the habit of doing, but let us encourage one another – and all the more as you see the Day approaching.

Hebrews 10:25

Cast your burden on the Lord, and he will sustain you; he will never permit the righteous to be moved.

Psalm 55:22 ESV

FAMILY

Good friend, follow your father's good advice; don't wander off from your mother's teachings. Wrap yourself in them from head to foot; wear them like a scarf around your neck. Wherever you walk, they'll guide you; whenever you rest, they'll guard you; when you wake up, they'll tell you what's next.

Proverbs 6:20-22 THE MESSAGE

So now Jesus and the ones he makes holy have the same Father. That is why Jesus is not ashamed to call them his brothers and sisters.

Hebrews 2:11 NLT

For my father and my mother have forsaken me, but the LORD will take me in.

Psalm 27:10 ESV

How great is the love the Father has lavished on us, that we should be called children of God! And that is what we are!

1 John 3:1

As a father has compassion on his children, so the LORD has compassion on those who fear him.

Psalm 103:13

For this reason I bow my knees to the Father of our Lord Jesus Christ, from whom the whole family in heaven and earth is named.

Ephesians 3:14-15 NKJV

"Honor your father and mother. Then you will live a long, full life in the land the LORD your God will give you."

Exodus 20:12 NLT

"Whoever does the will of God, he is my brother and sister and mother."

Mark 3:35 ESV

Train up a child in the way he should go, and when he is old he will not depart from it.

Proverbs 22:6 NKJV

When I left the womb you cradled me; since the moment of birth you've been my God.

Psalm 22:10 THE MESSAGE

"I will be a Father to you, and you will be my sons and daughters, says the Lord Almighty."

2 Corinthians 6:18

Father to the fatherless, defender of widows – this is God, whose dwelling is holy. God places the lonely in families; he sets the prisoners free and gives them joy.

Psalm 68:5-6 NLT

FORGIVENESS

If My people who are called by My name will humble themselves, and pray and seek My face, and turn from their wicked ways, then I will hear from heaven, and will forgive their sin and heal their land.

2 Chronicles 7:14 NKJV

"I will forgive their wrongdoings, and I will never again remember their sins," says the Lord.

Hebrews 8:12 NLT

You forgave the iniquity of your people; you covered all their sin.

Psalm 85:2 ESV

"For if you forgive men their trespasses, your heavenly Father will also forgive you. But if you do not forgive men their trespasses, neither will your Father forgive your trespasses."

Matthew 6:14-15 NKJV

If we confess our sins, he is faithful and just to forgive us our sins and to cleanse us from all unrighteousness.

1 John 1:9 ESV

You must make allowance for each other's faults and forgive the person who offends you. Remember, the Lord forgave you, so you must forgive others.

Colossians 3:13 NLT

"When you stand praying, if you hold anything against anyone, forgive him, so that your Father in heaven may forgive you your sins."

Mark 11:25

"Come now, let us reason together," says the LORD. "Though your sins are like scarlet, they shall be as white as snow; though they are red as crimson, they shall be like wool."

Isaiah 1:18

"I, even I, am He who blots out your transgressions for My own sake; and I will not remember your sins."

Isaiah 43:25 NKJV

In him we have redemption through his blood, the forgiveness of our trespasses, according to the riches of his grace.

Ephesians 1:7 ESV

"Give, and it will be given to you. A good measure, pressed down, shaken together and running over, will be poured into your lap. For with the measure you use, it will be measured to you."

Luke 6:38

God's Will

Trust in the Lord with all your heart and lean not on your own understanding; in all your ways acknowledge him, and he will make your paths straight.

Proverbs 3:5-6

He has showed you, O man, what is good. And what does the Lord require of you? To act justly and to love mercy and to walk humbly with your God.

Micah 6:8

Give thanks in all circumstances; for this is the will of God in Christ Jesus for you.

1 Thessalonians 5:18 ESV

If you call out for insight and cry aloud for understanding, and if you look for it as for silver and search for it as for hidden treasure, then you will understand the fear of the Lord and find the knowledge of God.

Proverbs 2:3-5

Do not be conformed to this world, but be transformed by the renewing of your mind, that you may prove what is that good and acceptable and perfect will of God.

Romans 12:2 NKJV

So if you are suffering according to God's will, keep on doing what is right, and trust yourself to the God who made you, for he will never fail you.

1 Peter 4:19 NLT

Jesus said to the people who believed in him, "You are truly my disciples if you keep obeying my teachings. And you will know the truth, and the truth will set you free."

John 8:31-32 NLT

The steps of the godly are directed by the LORD. He delights in every detail of their lives.

Psalm 37:23 NLT

It is God who works in you both to will and to do for His good pleasure.

Philippians 2:13 NKJV

"Here are My mother and My brothers! For whoever does the will of God is My brother and My sister and mother."

Mark 3:34-35 NKJV

"If anyone's will is to do God's will, he will know whether the teaching is from God or whether I am speaking on my own authority."

John 7:17 ESV

You need to persevere so that when you have done the will of God, you will receive what he has promised.

Hebrews 10:36

GRACE

We believe that through the grace of the Lord Jesus Christ we shall be saved in the same manner as they.

Acts 15:11 NKJV

Where sin increased, grace increased all the more.

Romans 5:20

God is able to make all grace abound toward you, that you, always having all sufficiency in all things, may have an abundance for every good work.

2 Corinthians 9:8 NKJV

For we do not have a high priest who is unable to sympathize with our weaknesses, but we have one who has been tempted in every way, just as we are – yet was without sin. Let us then approach the throne of grace with confidence, so that we may receive mercy and find grace to help us in our time of need.

Hebrews 4:15-16

For the grace of God has been revealed, bringing salvation to all people. And we are instructed to turn from godless living and sinful pleasures. We should live in this evil world with self-control, right conduct, and devotion to God, while we look forward to that wonderful event when the glory of our great God and Savior, Jesus Christ, will be revealed.

Titus 2:11-13 NLT

Therefore gird up the loins of your mind, be sober, and rest your hope fully upon the grace that is to be brought to you at the revelation of Jesus Christ.

1 Peter 1:13 NKJV

Therefore, since we have been made right in God's sight by faith, we have peace with God because of what Jesus Christ our Lord has done for us. Because of our faith, Christ has brought us into this place of highest privilege where we now stand, and we confidently and joyfully look forward to sharing God's glory.

Romans 5:1-2 NLT

"My gracious favor is all you need. My power works best in your weakness."

2 Corinthians 12:9 NLT

You know the grace of our Lord Jesus Christ, that though he was rich, yet for your sakes he became poor, so that you through his poverty might become rich.

2 Corinthians 8:9

"God opposes the proud, but gives grace to the humble."

James 4:6 ESV

GUIDANCE

This God is our God for ever and ever; he will be our guide even to the end.

Psalm 48:14

A man's heart plans his way, but the LORD directs his steps.

Proverbs 16:9 NKJV

I will lead the blind by ways they have not known, along unfamiliar paths I will guide them; I will turn the darkness into light before them and make the rough places smooth. These are the things I will do; I will not forsake them.

Isaiah 42:16

Trust in the Lord with all your heart, and lean not on your own understanding; in all your ways acknowledge Him, and He shall direct your paths.

Proverbs 3:5-6 NKJV

The steps of a man are established by the Lord, when he delights in his way.

Psalm 37:23 ESV

He will not let your foot slip – he who watches over you will not slumber; indeed, he who watches over Israel will neither slumber nor sleep. The Lord watches over you – the Lord is your shade at your right hand; the sun will not harm you by day, nor the moon by night.

Psalm 121:3-6

The Lord says, "I will guide you along the best pathway for your life. I will advise you and watch over you."

Psalm 32:8 NLT

For God's eyes are on the ways of a man, and he sees all his steps.

Job 34:21 ESV

Show me Your ways, O LORD; teach me Your paths. Lead me in Your truth and teach me, for You are the God of my salvation; on You I wait all the day.

Psalm 25:4-5 NKJV

You will hear a voice say, "This is the way; turn around and walk here."

Isaiah 30:21 NLT

Your word is a lamp to my feet and a light for my path.

Psalm 119:105

The righteousness of the blameless will direct his way aright, but the wicked will fall by his own wickedness.

Proverbs 11:5 NKJV

HAPPINESS

Is any one of you in trouble? He should pray. Is anyone happy? Let him sing songs of praise. Is any one of you sick? He should call the elders of the church to pray over him and anoint him with oil in the name of the Lord. And the prayer offered in faith will make the sick person well; the Lord will raise him up. If he has sinned, he will be forgiven.

James 5:13-15

I know the LORD is always with me. I will not be shaken, for he is right beside me. No wonder my heart is filled with joy, and my mouth shouts his praises!

Psalm 16:8-9 NLT

God gives wisdom, knowledge, and joy to those who please him.

Ecclesiastes 2:26 NLT

A happy heart makes the face cheerful, but heartache crushes the spirit.

Proverbs 15:13

Behold, happy is the man whom God corrects; therefore do not despise the chastening of the Almighty.

Job 5:17 NKJV

"His master replied, 'Well done, good and faithful servant! You have been faithful with a few things; I will put you in charge of many things. Come and share your master's happiness!'"

Matthew 25:23

Happy are those who fear the LORD. Yes, happy are those who delight in doing what he commands.

Psalm 112:1 NLT

You have made known to me the path of life; you will fill me with joy in your presence, with eternal pleasures at your right hand.

Psalm 16:11

Blessed is every one who fears the Lord, who walks in His ways. When you eat the labor of your hands, you shall be happy, and it shall be well with you.

Psalm 128:1-2 NKJV

Happy are those who have the God of Israel as their helper, whose hope is in the Lord their God.

Psalm 146:5 NLT

Happy is the person who finds wisdom and gains understanding. For the profit of wisdom is better than silver, and her wages are better than gold.

Proverbs 3:13-14 NLT

HELP

God is our refuge and strength, an ever-present help in trouble.

Psalm 46:1

The LORD is my strength and my shield; in him my heart trusts, and I am helped; my heart exults, and with my song I give thanks to him.

Psalm 28:7 ESV

"For You are my lamp, O LORD; the LORD shall enlighten my darkness. For by You I can run against a troop; by my God I can leap over a wall."

2 Samuel 22:29-30 NKJV

You will call, and the LORD will answer; you will cry for help, and he will say: Here am I.

Isaiah 58:9

I will lift up my eyes to the hills – from whence comes my help? My help comes from the LORD, who made heaven and earth.

Psalm 121:1-2 NKJV

The LORD is good, a stronghold in the day of trouble; and He knows those who trust in Him.

Nahum 1:7 NKJV

God will surely be gracious to you at the sound of your cry. As soon as he hears it, he answers you.

Isaiah 30:19 ESV

We depend on the LORD alone to save us. Only he can help us, protecting us like a shield.

Psalm 33:20 NLT

The Holy Spirit helps us in our distress. For we don't even know what we should pray for, nor how we should pray. But the Holy Spirit prays for us with groanings that cannot be expressed in words.

Romans 8:26 NLT

This is what the LORD says: "In the time of my favor I will answer you, and in the day of salvation I will help you; I will keep you and will make you to be a covenant for the people."

Isaiah 49:8

So let us come boldly to the throne of our gracious God. There we will receive his mercy, and we will find grace to help us when we need it.

Hebrews 4:16 NLT

Because you are my help, I sing in the shadow of your wings. My soul clings to you; your right hand upholds me.

Psalm 63:7-8

HOPE

Our hope is in the living God, who is the Savior of all people, and particularly of those who believe.

1 Timothy 4:10 NLT

Let us hold fast the confession of our hope without wavering, for He who promised is faithful.

Hebrews 10:23 NKJV

He delivered us from such a deadly peril, and he will deliver us. On him we have set our hope that he will deliver us again.

2 Corinthians 1:10 ESV

So be strong and take courage, all you who put your hope in the LORD!

Psalm 31:24 NLT

I pray also that the eyes of your heart may be enlightened in order that you may know the hope to which he has called you, the riches of his glorious inheritance in the saints, and his incomparably great power for us who believe. That power is like the working of his mighty strength.

Ephesians 1:18-19

Praise God, the Father of our Lord Jesus Christ. God is so good, and by raising Jesus from death, he has given us new life and a hope that lives on.

1 Peter 1:3 CEV

May the God of hope fill you with all joy and peace in believing, that you may abound in hope by the power of the Holy Spirit.

Romans 15:13 NKJV

There are three things that will endure –
faith, hope, and love.

1 Corinthians 13:13 NLT

For you, O Lord, are my hope, my trust, O
LORD, from my youth.

Psalm 71:5 ESV

For everything that was written in the past
was written to teach us, so that through
endurance and the encouragement of the
Scriptures we might have hope.

Romans 15:4

The LORD is good to those whose hope is in
him, to the one who seeks him.

Lamentations 3:25

To them God willed to make known what
are the riches of the glory of this mystery
among the Gentiles: which is Christ in you,
the hope of glory.

Colossians 1:27 NKJV

Integrity

As for me, You uphold me in my integrity, and set me before Your face forever.

Psalm 41:12 NKJV

The LORD God is a sun and shield; the LORD will give grace and glory; no good thing will He withhold from those who walk uprightly.

Psalm 84:11 NKJV

People with integrity have firm footing, but those who follow crooked paths will slip and fall.

Proverbs 10:9 NLT

Light dawns in the darkness for the upright;
he is gracious, merciful, and righteous.

Psalm 112:4 ESV

May integrity and honesty protect me, for
I put my hope in you.

Psalm 25:21 NLT

"By standing firm you will gain life."

Luke 21:19

He keeps his eye on all who live honestly,
and pays special attention to his loyally
committed ones.

Proverbs 2:8 THE MESSAGE

For only the upright will live in the land,
and those who have integrity will remain
in it.

Proverbs 2:21 NLT

Light is shed upon the righteous and joy on the upright in heart.

Psalm 97:11

May God himself, the God of peace, sanctify you through and through. May your whole spirit, soul and body be kept blameless at the coming of our Lord Jesus Christ. The one who calls you is faithful and he will do it.

1 Thessalonians 5:23-24

For the LORD is righteous; he loves righteous deeds; the upright shall behold his face.

Psalm 11:7 ESV

Good people are guided by their honesty; treacherous people are destroyed by their dishonesty.

Proverbs 11:3 NLT

LEADERSHIP

"Do not look at his appearance or at his physical stature, because I have refused him. For the LORD does not see as man sees; for man looks at the outward appearance, but the LORD looks at the heart."

1 Samuel 16:7 NKJV

"Now go; I will help you speak and will teach you what to say."

Exodus 4:12

Death and life are in the power of the tongue, and those who love it will eat its fruits.

Proverbs 18:21 ESV

If your gift is to encourage others, do it! If you have money, share it generously. If God has given you leadership ability, take the responsibility seriously. And if you have a gift for showing kindness to others, do it gladly.

Romans 12:8 NLT

Be shepherds of God's flock that is under your care, serving as overseers – not because you must, but because you are willing, as God wants you to be; not greedy for money, but eager to serve; not lording it over those entrusted to you, but being examples to the flock. And when the Chief Shepherd appears, you will receive the crown of glory that will never fade away.

1 Peter 5:2-4

Let no one despise you for your youth, but set the believers an example in speech, in conduct, in love, in faith, in purity. Persist in this, for by so doing you will save both yourself and your hearers.

1 Timothy 4:12, 16 ESV

He must manage his own family well and see that his children obey him with proper respect.

1 Timothy 3:4

Now give me wisdom and knowledge, that I may go out and come in before this people; for who can judge this great people of Yours?

2 Chronicles 1:10 NKJV

Remember your leaders, those who spoke to you the word of God. Consider the outcome of their way of life, and imitate their faith.

Hebrews 13:7 ESV

"Whoever wants to become great among you must be your servant, and whoever wants to be first must be slave of all. For even the Son of Man did not come to be served, but to serve, and to give his life as a ransom for many."

Mark 10:43-45

LOVE

"A new command I give you: Love one another. As I have loved you, so you must love one another. By this all men will know that you are my disciples, if you love one another."

John 13:34

As we live in God, our love grows more perfect. So we will not be afraid on the day of judgment, but we can face him with confidence because we are like Christ here in this world. Such love has no fear because perfect love expels all fear. If we are afraid, it is for fear of judgment, and this shows that his love has not been perfected in us.

1 John 4:17-18 NLT

Love each other deeply, because love covers over a multitude of sins.

1 Peter 4:8

The LORD appeared to him from far away. "I have loved you with an everlasting love; therefore I have continued my faithfulness to you."

Jeremiah 31:3 ESV

Eye has not seen, nor ear heard, nor have entered into the heart of man the things which God has prepared for those who love Him.

1 Corinthians 2:9 NKJV

For I am persuaded that neither death nor life, nor angels nor principalities nor powers, nor things present nor things to come, nor height nor depth, nor any other created thing, shall be able to separate us from the love of God which is in Christ Jesus our Lord.

Romans 8:38-39 NKJV

I love those who love me; those who look for me find me.

Proverbs 8:17 THE MESSAGE

The love of God has been poured out in our hearts by the Holy Spirit who was given to us.

Romans 5:5 NKJV

Everyone who believes that Jesus is the Christ is a child of God. And everyone who loves the Father loves his children, too. We know we love God's children if we love God and obey his commandments.

1 John 5:1-2 NLT

I, the LORD your God, am a jealous God who will not share your affection with any other god! I do not leave unpunished the sins of those who hate me. But I lavish my love on those who love me and obey my commands, even for a thousand generations.

Exodus 20:5-6 NLT

Marriage

Wives, submit to your husbands as to the Lord. For the husband is the head of the wife as Christ is the head of the church, his body, of which he is the Savior. Now as the church submits to Christ, so also wives should submit to their husbands in everything.

Ephesians 5:22-24

"'For this reason a man will leave his father and mother and be united to his wife, and the two will become one flesh.' So they are no longer two, but one. Therefore what God has joined together, let man not separate."

Mark 10:7-9

A man will leave his father and mother and be united to his wife, and the two will become one flesh.

Ephesians 5:31

Confess your trespasses to one another, and pray for one another, that you may be healed.

James 5:16 NKJV

He who finds a wife finds a good thing, and obtains favor from the LORD.

Proverbs 18:22 NKJV

Parents can provide their sons with an inheritance of houses and wealth, but only the LORD can give an understanding wife.

Proverbs 19:14 NLT

Give honor to marriage, and remain faithful to one another in marriage. God will surely judge people who are immoral and those who commit adultery.

Hebrews 13:4 NLT

Let the husband render to his wife the affection due her, and likewise also the wife to her husband.

1 Corinthians 7:3 NKJV

To the married I give this charge (not I, but the Lord): the wife should not separate from her husband.

1 Corinthians 7:10 ESV

Husbands, live with your wives in an understanding way, showing honor to the woman as the weaker vessel, since they are heirs with you of the grace of life.

1 Peter 3:7 ESV

A hearty wife invigorates her husband, but a frigid woman is cancer in the bones.

Proverbs 12:4 THE MESSAGE

Charm is deceitful, and beauty is vain, but a woman who fears the LORD is to be praised.

Proverbs 31:30 ESV

Modesty

Do not be rash with your mouth, and let not your heart utter anything hastily before God. For God is in heaven, and you on earth; therefore let your words be few.

Ecclesiastes 5:2 NKJV

Don't call attention to yourself; let others do that for you.

Proverbs 27:2 THE MESSAGE

Do not deceive yourselves. If any one of you thinks he is wise by the standards of this age, he should become a "fool" so that he may become wise.

1 Corinthians 3:18

Pride ends in humiliation, while humility brings honor.

Proverbs 29:23 NLT

The meek shall obtain fresh joy in the LORD, and the poor among mankind shall exult in the Holy One of Israel.

Isaiah 29:19 ESV

God gives us more grace. That is why Scripture says: "God opposes the proud but gives grace to the humble."

James 4:6

As it is, you boast in your arrogance. All such boasting is evil.

James 4:16 ESV

"Whoever humbles himself like this child is the greatest in the kingdom of heaven."

Matthew 18:4

Humble yourselves, therefore, under God's mighty hand, that he may lift you up in due time.

1 Peter 5:6

"Take care! Don't do your good deeds publicly, to be admired, because then you will lose the reward from your Father in heaven."

Matthew 6:1 NLT

Do not boast about tomorrow, for you do not know what a day may bring.

Proverbs 27:1 ESV

He chose the lowly things of this world and the despised things – and the things that are not – to nullify the things that are, so that no one may boast before him.

1 Corinthians 1:28-29

PATIENCE

Dear brothers, you must be patient as you wait for the Lord's return. Consider the farmers who eagerly look for the rains in the fall and in the spring. They patiently wait for the precious harvest to ripen. You, too, must be patient. And take courage, for the coming of the Lord is near.

James 5:7-8 NLT

My brethren, count it all joy when you fall into various trials, knowing that the testing of your faith produces patience. But let patience have its perfect work, that you may be perfect and complete, lacking nothing.

James 1:2-4 NKJV

But those who wait on the LORD shall renew their strength; they shall mount up with wings like eagles, they shall run and not be weary, they shall walk and not faint.

Isaiah 40:31 NKJV

You may not be sluggish, but imitators of those who through faith and patience inherit the promises.

Hebrews 6:12 ESV

I waited patiently for the LORD to help me, and he turned to me and heard my cry.

Psalm 40:1 NLT

Be patient and stand firm, because the Lord's coming is near.

James 5:8

For the revelation awaits an appointed time; it speaks of the end and will not prove false. Though it linger, wait for it; it will certainly come and will not delay.

Habakkuk 2:3

Always be humble and gentle. Patiently put up with each other and love each other.

Ephesians 4:2 CEV

Rest in the LORD, and wait patiently for Him; do not fret because of him who prospers in his way.

Psalm 37:7 NKJV

Patient endurance is what you need now, so you will continue to do God's will. Then you will receive all that he has promised.

Hebrews 10:36 NLT

Let us not become weary in doing good, for at the proper time we will reap a harvest if we do not give up.

Galatians 6:9

The LORD is good to those who wait for him, to the soul who seeks him.

Lamentations 3:25 ESV

PERSEVERANCE

We also rejoice in our sufferings, because we know that suffering produces perseverance; perseverance, character; and character, hope. And hope does not disappoint us, because God has poured out his love into our hearts by the Holy Spirit, whom he has given us.

Romans 5:3-5

"Because you have obeyed my command to persevere, I will protect you from the great time of testing that will come upon the whole world to test those who belong to this world."

Revelation 3:10 NLT

"Be strong and do not let your hands be weak, for your work shall be rewarded!"

2 Chronicles 15:7 NKJV

Let us throw off everything that hinders and the sin that so easily entangles, and let us run with perseverance the race marked out for us.

Hebrews 12:1

You need to persevere so that when you have done the will of God, you will receive what he has promised.

Hebrews 10:36

For we share in Christ, if indeed we hold our original confidence firm to the end.

Hebrews 3:14 ESV

Let us not grow weary while doing good, for in due season we shall reap if we do not lose heart.

Galatians 6:9 NKJV

"The one who endures to the end will be saved."

Matthew 24:13 ESV

Blessed is the man who endures temptation; for when he has been approved, he will receive the crown of life which the Lord has promised to those who love Him.

James 1:12 NKJV

"Everyone will hate you because of your allegiance to me. But those who endure to the end will be saved."

Matthew 10:22 NLT

Therefore, be steadfast, immovable, always abounding in the work of the Lord, knowing that in the Lord your labor is not in vain.

1 Corinthians 15:58 ESV

All who win the victory will be given these blessings. I will be their God, and they will be my people.

Revelation 21:7 CEV

Prayer

"It shall come to pass that before they call, I will answer; and while they are still speaking, I will hear."

Isaiah 65:24 NKJV

"In those days when you pray, I will listen. If you look for me in earnest, you will find me when you seek me."

Jeremiah 29:12-13 NLT

"When you pray, go into your room, close the door and pray to your Father, who is unseen. Then your Father, who sees what is done in secret, will reward you."

Matthew 6:6

"Whatever you ask in prayer, you will receive, if you have faith."

Matthew 21:22 ESV

While Jesus was here on earth, he offered prayers and pleadings, with a loud cry and tears, to the one who could deliver him out of death. And God heard his prayers because of his reverence for God.

Hebrews 5:7 NLT

The LORD is near to all who call on him, to all who call on him in truth. He fulfills the desires of those who fear him; he hears their cry and saves them.

Psalm 145:18-19

"Call upon me in the day of trouble; I will deliver you, and you will honor me."

Psalm 50:15

The earnest prayer of a righteous person has great power and wonderful results.

James 5:16 NLT

Be anxious for nothing, but in everything by prayer and supplication, with thanksgiving, let your requests be made known to God; and the peace of God, which surpasses all understanding, will guard your hearts and minds through Christ Jesus.

Philippians 4:6-7 NKJV

"I say to you, whatever things you ask when you pray, believe that you receive them, and you will have them."

Mark 11:24 NKJV

"Truly, truly, I say to you, whatever you ask of the Father in my name, he will give it to you. Until now you have asked nothing in my name. Ask, and you will receive, that your joy may be full."

John 16:23-24 ESV

For the eyes of the Lord are on the righteous and his ears are attentive to their prayer.

1 Peter 3:12

PROTECTION

The name of the LORD is a strong tower; the righteous man runs into it and is safe.

Proverbs 18:10 ESV

The LORD keeps you from all evil and preserves your life. The LORD keeps watch over you as you come and go, both now and forever.

Psalm 121:7-8 NLT

The Lord is faithful, and he will strengthen and protect you from the evil one.

2 Thessalonians 3:3

The LORD is my light and my salvation; whom shall I fear? The LORD is the strength of my life; of whom shall I be afraid?

Psalm 27:1-2 NKJV

The angel of the LORD guards all who fear him, and he rescues them.

Psalm 34:7 NLT

"The beloved of the LORD dwells in safety. The High God surrounds him all day long, and dwells between his shoulders."

Deuteronomy 33:12 ESV

When you lie down, you will not be afraid; when you lie down, your sleep will be sweet.

Proverbs 3:24

So do not fear, for I am with you; do not be dismayed, for I am your God. I will strengthen you and help you; I will uphold you with my righteous right hand.

Isaiah 41:10

He who dwells in the secret place of the Most High shall abide under the shadow of the Almighty. I will say of the LORD, "He is my refuge and my fortress; my God, in Him I will trust."

Psalm 91:1-2 NKJV

We know that those who have become part of God's family do not make a practice of sinning, for God's Son holds them securely, and the evil one cannot get his hands on them.

1 John 5:18 NLT

Blessed is the one who considers the poor! In the day of trouble the LORD delivers him; the LORD protects him and keeps him alive; he is called blessed in the land.

Psalm 41:1-2 ESV

The LORD preserves the simple; I was brought low, and He saved me.

Psalm 116:6 NKJV

Provision

The LORD is my shepherd, I shall not be in want.

Psalm 23:1

His divine power has granted to us all things that pertain to life and godliness, through the knowledge of him who called us to his own glory and excellence, by which he has granted to us his precious and very great promises.

2 Peter 1:3-4 ESV

"Your Father knows the things you have need of before you ask Him."

Matthew 6:8 NKJV

The LORD bestows favor and honor. No good thing does he withhold from those who walk uprightly.

Psalm 84:11 ESV

My God will meet all your needs according to his glorious riches in Christ Jesus.

Philippians 4:19

Sloth makes you poor; diligence brings wealth.

Proverbs 10:4 THE MESSAGE

"I will raise up for them a garden of renown, and they shall no longer be consumed with hunger in the land, nor bear the shame of the Gentiles anymore. Thus they shall know that I, the LORD their God, am with them."

Ezekiel 34:29-30 NKJV

He will give grass in your fields for your livestock, and you shall eat and be full.

Deuteronomy 11:15 ESV

For even when we were with you, we gave you this rule: "If a man will not work, he shall not eat."

2 Thessalonians 3:10

But if anyone does not provide for his own, and especially for those of his household, he has denied the faith and is worse than an unbeliever.

1 Timothy 5:8 NKJV

Don't forget to do good and to share what you have with those in need, for such sacrifices are very pleasing to God.

Hebrews 13:16 NLT

Jesus replied, "I am the bread of life. No one who comes to me will ever be hungry again."

John 6:35 NLT

REST

"Come to me, all you who are weary and burdened, and I will give you rest. Take my yoke upon you and learn from me, for I am gentle and humble in heart, and you will find rest for your souls."

Matthew 11:28-29

"In returning and rest you shall be saved; in quietness and in trust shall be your strength."

Isaiah 30:15 ESV

"My Presence will go with you, and I will give you rest."

Exodus 33:14 NKJV

"The LORD your God in your midst, the Mighty One, will save; He will rejoice over you with gladness, He will quiet you with His love, He will rejoice over you with singing."

Zephaniah 3:17 NKJV

My people will live in safety, quietly at home. They will be at rest.

Isaiah 32:18 NLT

My soul finds rest in God alone; my salvation comes from him. He alone is my rock and my salvation; he is my fortress, I will never be shaken.

Psalm 62:1-2

You let me rest in fields of green grass. You lead me to streams of peaceful water, and you refresh my life. You are true to your name, and you lead me along the right paths.

Psalm 23:2-3 CEV

"The LORD himself will fight for you. You won't have to lift a finger in your defense!"

Exodus 14:14 NLT

He who dwells in the shelter of the Most High will rest in the shadow of the Almighty. I will say of the LORD, "He is my refuge and my fortress, my God, in whom I trust."

Psalm 91:1-2

"Stand in the ways and see, and ask for the old paths, where the good way is, and walk in it; then you will find rest for your souls."

Jeremiah 6:16 NKJV

The fear of the LORD leads to life, and whoever has it rests satisfied; he will not be visited by harm.

Proverbs 19:23 ESV

I will lie down and sleep in peace, for you alone, O LORD, make me dwell in safety.

Psalm 4:8

Satisfaction

Command those who are rich in this present age not to be haughty, nor to trust in uncertain riches but in the living God, who gives us richly all things to enjoy. Let them do good, that they be rich in good works, ready to give, willing to share, storing up for themselves a good foundation for the time to come, that they may lay hold on eternal life.

1 Timothy 6:17-19 NKJV

Let them give thanks to the LORD for his unfailing love and his wonderful deeds for men, for he satisfies the thirsty and fills the hungry with good things.

Psalm 107:8-9

Satisfy us in the morning with your steadfast love, that we may rejoice and be glad all our days.

Psalm 90:14 ESV

You open your hand and satisfy the desires of every living thing.

Psalm 145:16

"God blesses those who are hungry and thirsty for justice, for they will receive it in full."

Matthew 5:6 NLT

Delight yourself also in the LORD, and He shall give you the desires of your heart.

Psalm 37:4 NKJV

"Whoever drinks of the water that I will give him will never be thirsty forever. The water that I will give him will become in him a spring of water welling up to eternal life."

John 4:14 ESV

True religion with contentment is great wealth. After all, we didn't bring anything with us when we came into the world, and we certainly cannot carry anything with us when we die. So if we have enough food and clothing, let us be content.

1 Timothy 6:6-8 NLT

Jesus said to them, "I am the bread of life. He who comes to Me shall never hunger, and he who believes in Me shall never thirst."

John 6:35 NKJV

My soul will be satisfied as with the richest of foods; with singing lips my mouth will praise you.

Psalm 63:5

Keep your lives free from the love of money and be content with what you have, because God has said, "Never will I leave you; never will I forsake you."

Hebrews 13:5

SELF-CONTROL

Above all else, guard your heart, for it affects everything you do.

Proverbs 4:23 NLT

Whoever guards his mouth and tongue keeps his soul from troubles.

Proverbs 21:23 NKJV

It teaches us to say "No" to ungodliness and worldly passions, and to live self-controlled, upright and godly lives in this present age, while we wait for the blessed hope – the glorious appearing of our great God and Savior, Jesus Christ.

Titus 2:12-13

Every athlete exercises self-control in all things. They do it to receive a perishable wreath, but we an imperishable.

1 Corinthians 9:25 ESV

Knowing God leads to self-control. Self-control leads to patient endurance, and patient endurance leads to godliness.

2 Peter 1:6 NLT

Prepare your minds for action; be self-controlled; set your hope fully on the grace to be given you when Jesus Christ is revealed.

1 Peter 1:13

Let the Lord Jesus Christ take control of you, and don't think of ways to indulge your evil desires.

Romans 13:14 NLT

Whoever has no rule over his own spirit is like a city broken down, without walls.

Proverbs 25:28 NKJV

For God gave us a spirit not of fear but of power and love and self-control.

2 Timothy 1:7 ESV

Brothers, you have no obligation whatsoever to do what your sinful nature urges you to do. For if you keep on following it, you will perish. But if through the power of the Holy Spirit you turn from it and its evil deeds, you will live.

Romans 8:12-13 NLT

A man of knowledge uses words with restraint, and a man of understanding is even-tempered.

Proverbs 17:27

When you're given a box of candy, don't gulp it all down; eat too much chocolate and you'll make yourself sick.

Proverbs 25:16 THE MESSAGE

STRENGTH

I can do all things through Christ who strengthens me.

Philippians 4:13 NKJV

The LORD gives strength to his people; the LORD blesses his people with peace.

Psalm 29:11

God gives power to the faint, and to him who has no might he increases strength.

Isaiah 40:29 ESV

My health may fail, and my spirit may grow weak, but God remains the strength of my heart.

Psalm 73:26 NLT

"My grace is sufficient for you, for My strength is made perfect in weakness."

2 Corinthians 12:9 NKJV

Those who hope in the LORD will renew their strength. They will soar on wings like eagles; they will run and not grow weary, they will walk and not be faint.

Isaiah 40:31

For you equipped me with strength for the battle; you made those who rise against me sink under me.

2 Samuel 22:40 ESV

Happy are those who are strong in the LORD, who set their minds on a pilgrimage to Jerusalem.

Psalm 84:5 NLT

The LORD is my strength and my song, and he has become my salvation.

Exodus 15:2 ESV

Go and enjoy choice food and sweet drinks, and send some to those who have nothing prepared. This day is sacred to our LORD. Do not grieve, for the joy of the LORD is your strength.

Nehemiah 8:10

God is my strength and power, and He makes my way perfect. He makes my feet like the feet of deer, and sets me on my high places.

2 Samuel 22:33-34 NKJV

"My gracious favor is all you need. My power works best in your weakness." So now I am glad to boast about my weaknesses, so that the power of Christ may work through me.

2 Corinthians 12:9 NLT

Success

The LORD will grant you abundant prosperity – in the fruit of your womb, the young of your livestock and the crops of your ground – in the land he swore to your forefathers to give you. The LORD will open the heavens, the storehouse of his bounty, to send rain on your land in season and to bless all the work of your hands.

Deuteronomy 28:11-12

Wealth and glory accompany me – also substantial Honor and a Good Name. My benefits are worth more than a big salary, even a *very* big salary; the returns on me exceed any imaginable bonus.

Proverbs 8:18-19 THE MESSAGE

Slaves, obey your earthly masters with respect and fear, and with sincerity of heart, just as you would obey Christ. Serve wholeheartedly, as if you were serving the Lord, not men, because you know that the Lord will reward everyone for whatever good he does, whether he is slave or free.

Ephesians 6:5, 7-8

It is not that we think we can do anything of lasting value by ourselves. Our only power and success come from God.

2 Corinthians 3:5 NLT

The reward for humility and fear of the LORD is riches and honor and life.

Proverbs 22:4 ESV

This Book of the Law shall not depart from your mouth, but you shall meditate in it day and night, that you may observe to do according to all that is written in it. For then you will make your way prosperous, and then you will have good success.

Joshua 1:8 NKJV

"I know the plans I have for you," declares the LORD, "plans to prosper you and not to harm you, plans to give you hope and a future."

Jeremiah 29:11

David had success in all his undertakings, for the LORD was with him.

1 Samuel 18:14 ESV

Command those who are rich in this present age not to be haughty, nor to trust in uncertain riches but in the living God, who gives us richly all things to enjoy.

1 Timothy 6:17 NKJV

Jesus said, "With man this is impossible, but with God all things are possible."

Matthew 19:26 ESV

The generous prosper and are satisfied; those who refresh others will themselves be refreshed.

Proverbs 11:25 NLT

TRUST

The LORD is good. When trouble comes, he is a strong refuge. And he knows everyone who trusts in him.

Nahum 1:7 NLT

Trust in the LORD, and do good; dwell in the land and befriend faithfulness. Delight yourself in the LORD, and he will give you the desires of your heart.

Psalm 37:3-4 ESV

Those who know your name will trust in you, for you, LORD, have never forsaken those who seek you.

Psalm 9:10

Blessed are all those who put their trust in Him.

Psalm 2:12 NKJV

Trust in the LORD with all your heart, and lean not on your own understanding; in all your ways acknowledge Him, and He shall direct your paths.

Proverbs 3:5-6 NKJV

I trust in God, so why should I be afraid? What can mere mortals do to me?

Psalm 56:11 NLT

Trust in Him at all times, you people; pour out your heart before Him; God is a refuge for us.

Psalm 62:8 NKJV

May the God of hope fill you with all joy and peace as you trust in him, so that you may overflow with hope by the power of the Holy Spirit.

Romans 15:13

Behold, God is my salvation; I will trust, and will not be afraid; for the LORD GOD is my strength and my song, and he has become my salvation.

Isaiah 12:2 ESV

"See, I lay a stone in Zion, a chosen and precious cornerstone, and the one who trusts in him will never be put to shame."

1 Peter 2:6

For to this end we both labor and suffer reproach, because we trust in the living God, who is the Savior of all men, especially of those who believe.

1 Timothy 4:10 NKJV

Surely this is our God; we trusted in him, and he saved us. This is the LORD, we trusted in him; let us rejoice and be glad in his salvation.

Isaiah 25:9

Wealth

But seek first the kingdom of God and His righteousness, and all these things shall be added to you.

Matthew 6:33 NKJV

You will prosper, if you take care to fulfill the statutes and judgments with which the LORD charged Moses concerning Israel. Be strong and of good courage.

1 Chronicles 22:13 NKJV

"Take care, and be on your guard against all covetousness, for one's life does not consist in the abundance of his possessions."

Luke 12:15 ESV

Now there is great gain in godliness with contentment, for we brought nothing into the world, and we cannot take anything out of the world. But if we have food and clothing, with these we will be content.

1 Timothy 6:6-8 ESV

Give great joy to those who have stood with me in my defense. Let them continually say, "Great is the LORD, who enjoys helping his servant."

Psalm 35:27 NLT

It is a good thing to receive wealth from God and the good health to enjoy it. To enjoy your work and accept your lot in life – that is indeed a gift from God.

Ecclesiastes 5:19 NLT

God doesn't care how great a person may be, and he doesn't pay any more attention to the rich than to the poor. He made them all.

Job 34:19 NLT

If they obey and serve God, they will spend the rest of their days in prosperity and their years in contentment.

Job 36:11

Keep the words of this covenant and do them, that you may prosper in all that you do.

Deuteronomy 29:9 ESV

A faithful man will be richly blessed, but one eager to get rich will not go unpunished.

Proverbs 28:20

Make it your ambition to lead a quiet life, to mind your own business and to work with your hands, just as we told you, so that your daily life may win the respect of outsiders and so that you will not be dependent on anybody.

1 Thessalonians 4:11-12

WISDOM

To the man who pleases him, God gives wisdom, knowledge and happiness.

Ecclesiastes 2:26

If you need wisdom – if you want to know what God wants you to do – ask him, and he will gladly tell you. He will not resent your asking.

James 1:5 NLT

Wisdom and knowledge will be the stability of your times, and the strength of salvation; the fear of the LORD is His treasure.

Isaiah 33:6 NKJV

The fear of the LORD is the beginning of wisdom; a good understanding have all those who do His commandments. His praise endures forever.

Psalm 111:10 NKJV

Wisdom strengthens the wise more than ten rulers of the city.

Ecclesiastes 7:19 NKJV

A wise man is full of strength, and a man of knowledge enhances his might, for by wise guidance you can wage your war and in abundance of counselors there is victory.

Proverbs 24:5-6 ESV

Wisdom is sweet to your soul. If you find it, you will have a bright future, and your hopes will not be cut short.

Proverbs 24:14 NLT

The fruit of the righteous is a tree of life, and he who wins souls is wise.

Proverbs 11:30

Happy is the person who finds wisdom and gains understanding. For the profit of wisdom is better than silver, and her wages are better than gold.

Proverbs 3:13-14 NLT

In him we have redemption through his blood, the forgiveness of sins, in accordance with the riches of God's grace that he lavished on us with all wisdom and understanding.

Ephesians 1:7-8

But the wisdom from above is first pure, then peaceable, gentle, open to reason, full of mercy and good fruits, impartial and sincere. And a harvest of righteousness is sown in peace by those who make peace.

James 3:17-18 ESV

Oh, the depth of the riches of the wisdom and knowledge of God! How unsearchable his judgments, and his paths beyond tracing out!

Romans 11:33

WORK

God has promised us a Sabbath when we will rest, even though it has not yet come. On that day God's people will rest from their work, just as God rested from his work.

Hebrews 4:9-10 CEV

"His lord said to him, 'Well done, good and faithful servant; you have been faithful over a few things, I will make you ruler over many things. Enter into the joy of your lord.'"

Matthew 25:23 NKJV

Whatever you do, do well. For when you go to the grave, there will be no work or planning or knowledge or wisdom.

Ecclesiastes 9:10 NLT

Jesus said, "Do not labor for the food which perishes, but for the food which endures to everlasting life, which the Son of Man will give you, because God the Father has set His seal on Him."

John 6:27 NKJV

Therefore, my beloved brethren, be steadfast, immovable, always abounding in the work of the Lord, knowing that your labor is not in vain in the Lord.

1 Corinthians 15:58 NKJV

Do your best to present yourself to God as one approved, a worker who has no need to be ashamed, rightly handling the word of truth.

2 Timothy 2:15 ESV

The LORD will open the heavens, the store-house of his bounty, to send rain on your land in season and to bless all the work of your hands.

Deuteronomy 28:12

Whatever you do, work at it with all your heart, as working for the Lord, not for men, since you know that you will receive an inheritance from the Lord as a reward. It is the Lord Christ you are serving.

Colossians 3:23-24

The man who plants and the man who waters have one purpose, and each will be rewarded according to his own labor.

1 Corinthians 3:8

Don't just do what you have to do to get by, but work heartily. And work with a smile on your face, always keeping in mind that no matter who happens to be giving the orders, you're really serving God.

Ephesians 6:7-8 THE MESSAGE

WORRY

Worry weighs a person down; an encouraging word cheers a person up.

Proverbs 12:25 NLT

God is greater than our worried hearts and knows more about us than we do ourselves.

1 John 3:20 THE MESSAGE

It is the LORD who goes before you. He will be with you; he will not leave you or forsake you. Do not fear or be dismayed.

Deuteronomy 31:8 ESV

Do not be anxious about anything, but in everything, by prayer and petition, with thanksgiving, present your requests to God. And the peace of God, which transcends all understanding, will guard your hearts and your minds in Christ Jesus.

Philippians 4:6-7

For God did not give us a spirit of timidity, but a spirit of power, of love and of self-discipline.

2 Timothy 1:7

Though I walk in the midst of trouble, you preserve my life; you stretch out your hand against the wrath of my enemies, and your right hand delivers me.

Psalm 138:7 ESV

"For the mountains shall depart and the hills be removed, but My kindness shall not depart from you, nor shall My covenant of peace be removed," says the LORD, who has mercy on you.

Isaiah 54:10 NKJV

When doubts filled my mind, your comfort gave me renewed hope and cheer.

Psalm 94:19 NLT

Cast all your anxiety on him because he cares for you.

1 Peter 5:7

"Seek first the kingdom of God and His righteousness, and all these things shall be added to you. Therefore do not worry about tomorrow, for tomorrow will worry about its own things. Sufficient for the day is its own trouble."

Matthew 6:33-34 NKJV

The Lord is my helper, so I will not be afraid. What can mere mortals do to me?

Hebrews 13:6 NLT

Cast your burden on the LORD, and He shall sustain you; He shall never permit the righteous to be moved.

Psalm 55:22 NKJV

WORSHIP

Therefore, since we are receiving a kingdom that cannot be shaken, let us be thankful, and so worship God acceptably with reverence and awe, for our "God is a consuming fire."

Hebrews 12:28-29

"God is spirit, and his worshipers must worship in spirit and in truth."

John 4:24

You must worship no other gods, but only the LORD, for he is a God who is passionate about his relationship with you.

Exodus 34:14 NLT

I will thank you forever, because you have done it. I will wait for your name, for it is good, in the presence of the godly.

Psalm 52:9 ESV

I praise you because I am fearfully and wonderfully made; your works are wonderful, I know that full well.

Psalm 139:14

For great is the LORD, and greatly to be praised, and he is to be held in awe above all gods.

1 Chronicles 16:25 ESV

Give honor to the LORD for the glory of his name. Worship the LORD in the splendor of his holiness.

Psalm 29:2 NLT

Great is the LORD! He is most worthy of praise! He is to be revered above all the gods.

Psalm 96:4 NLT

Blessed be the God and Father of our Lord Jesus Christ, who according to His abundant mercy has begotten us again to a living hope through the resurrection of Jesus Christ from the dead.

1 Peter 1:3 NKJV

Take your everyday, ordinary life – your sleeping, eating, going-to-work, and walking-around life – and place it before God as an offering. Embracing what God does for you is the best thing you can do for him.

Romans 12:1 THE MESSAGE

The LORD lives! Praise be to my Rock! Exalted be God, the Rock, my Savior!

2 Samuel 22:47-48

Praise be to the God and Father of our Lord Jesus Christ, who has blessed us in the heavenly realms with every spiritual blessing in Christ. For he chose us in him before the creation of the world to be holy and blameless in his sight.

Ephesians 1:3-4

One Year Bible Reading Plan

January

1 Genesis 1-2; Psalm 1; Matthew 1-2
2 Genesis 3-4; Psalm 2; Matthew 3-4
3 Genesis 5-7; Psalm 3; Matthew 5
4 Genesis 8-9; Psalm 4; Matthew 6-7
5 Genesis 10-11; Psalm 5; Matthew 8-9
6 Genesis 12-13; Psalm 6; Matthew 10-11
7 Genesis 14-15; Psalm 7; Matthew 12
8 Genesis 16-17; Psalm 8; Matthew 13
9 Genesis 18-19; Psalm 9; Matthew 14-15
10 Genesis 20-21; Psalm 10; Matthew 16-17
11 Genesis 22-23; Psalm 11; Matthew 18
12 Genesis 24; Psalm 12; Matthew 19-20
13 Genesis 25-26; Psalm 13; Matthew 21
14 Genesis 27-28; Psalm 14; Matthew 22
15 Genesis 29-30; Psalm 15; Matthew 23
16 Genesis 31-32; Psalm 16; Matthew 24
17 Genesis 33-34; Psalm 17; Matthew 25
18 Genesis 35-36; Psalm 18; Matthew 26
19 Genesis 37-38; Psalm 19; Matthew 27
20 Genesis 39-40; Psalm 20; Matthew 28
21 Genesis 41-42; Psalm 21; Mark 1
22 Genesis 43-44; Psalm 22; Mark 2
23 Genesis 45-46; Psalm 23; Mark 3
24 Genesis 47-48; Psalm 24; Mark 4
25 Genesis 49-50; Psalm 25; Mark 5
26 Exodus 1-2; Psalm 26; Mark 6
27 Exodus 3-4; Psalm 27; Mark 7
28 Exodus 5-6; Psalm 28; Mark 8
29 Exodus 7-8; Psalm 29; Mark 9
30 Exodus 9-10; Psalm 30; Mark 10
31 Exodus 11-12; Psalm 31; Mark 11

FEBRUARY

1   Exodus 13-14; Psalm 32; Mark 12
2   Exodus 15-16; Psalm 33; Mark 13
3   Exodus 17-18; Psalm 34; Mark 14
4   Exodus 19-20; Psalm 35; Mark 15
5   Exodus 21-22; Psalm 36; Mark 16
6   Exodus 23-24; Psalm 37; Luke 1
7   Exodus 25-26; Psalm 38; Luke 2
8   Exodus 27-28; Psalm 39; Luke 3
9   Exodus 29-30; Psalm 40; Luke 4
10 Exodus 31-32; Psalm 41; Luke 5
11 Exodus 33-34; Psalm 42; Luke 6
12 Exodus 35-36; Psalm 43; Luke 7
13 Exodus 37-38; Psalm 44; Luke 8
14 Exodus 39-40; Psalm 45; Luke 9
15 Leviticus 1-2; Psalm 46; Luke 10
16 Leviticus 3-4; Psalm 47; Luke 11
17 Leviticus 5-6; Psalm 48; Luke 12
18 Leviticus 7-8; Psalm 49; Luke 13
19 Leviticus 9-10; Psalm 50; Luke 14
20 Leviticus 11-12; Psalm 51; Luke 15
21 Leviticus 13; Psalm 52; Luke 16
22 Leviticus 14; Psalm 53; Luke 17
23 Leviticus 15-16; Psalm 54; Luke 18
24 Leviticus 17-18; Psalm 55; Luke 19
25 Leviticus 19-20; Psalm 56; Luke 20
26 Leviticus 21-22; Psalm 57; Luke 21
27 Leviticus 23-24; Psalm 58; Luke 22
28 Leviticus 25; Psalm 59; Luke 23

March

1   Leviticus 26-27; Psalm 60; Luke 24
2   Numbers 1-2; Psalm 61; John 1
3   Numbers 3-4; Psalm 62; John 2-3
4   Numbers 5-6; Psalm 63; John 4
5   Numbers 7; Psalm 64; John 5
6   Numbers 8-9; Psalm 65; John 6
7   Numbers 10-11; Psalm 66; John 7
8   Numbers 12-13; Psalm 67; John 8
9   Numbers 14-15; Psalm 68; John 9
10   Numbers 16; Psalm 69; John 10
11   Numbers 17-18; Psalm 70; John 11
12   Numbers 19-20; Psalm 71; John 12
13   Numbers 21-22; Psalm 72; John 13
14   Numbers 23-24; Psalm 73; John 14-15
15   Numbers 25-26; Psalm 74; John 16
16   Numbers 27-28; Psalm 75; John 17
17   Numbers 29-30; Psalm 76; John 18
18   Numbers 31-32; Psalm 77; John 19
19   Numbers 33-34; Psalm 78; John 20
20   Numbers 35-36; Psalm 79; John 21
21   Deuteronomy 1-2; Psalm 80; Acts 1
22   Deuteronomy 3-4; Psalm 81; Acts 2
23   Deuteronomy 5-6; Psalm 82; Acts 3-4
24   Deuteronomy 7-8; Psalm 83; Acts 5-6
25   Deuteronomy 9-10; Psalm 84; Acts 7
26   Deuteronomy 11-12; Psalm 85; Acts 8
27   Deuteronomy 13-14; Psalm 86; Acts 9
28   Deuteronomy 15-16; Psalm 87; Acts 10
29   Deuteronomy 17-18; Psalm 88; Acts 11-12
30   Deuteronomy 19-20; Psalm 89; Acts 13
31   Deuteronomy 21-22; Psalm 90; Acts 14

APRIL

1 Deuteronomy 23-24; Psalm 91; Acts 15
2 Deuteronomy 25-27; Psalm 92; Acts 16
3 Deuteronomy 28-29; Psalm 93; Acts 17
4 Deuteronomy 30-31; Psalm 94; Acts 18
5 Deuteronomy 32; Psalm 95; Acts 19
6 Deuteronomy, 33-34; Psalm 96; Acts 20
7 Joshua 1-2; Psalm 97; Acts 21
8 Joshua 3-4; Psalm 98; Acts 22
9 Joshua 5-6; Psalm 99; Acts 23
10 Joshua 7-8; Psalm 100; Acts 24-25
11 Joshua 9-10; Psalm 101; Acts 26
12 Joshua 11-12; Psalm 102; Acts 27
13 Joshua 13-14; Psalm 103; Acts 28
14 Joshua 15-16; Psalm 104; Romans 1-2
15 Joshua 17-18; Psalm 105; Romans 3-4
16 Joshua 19-20; Psalm 106; Romans 5-6
17 Joshua 21-22; Psalm 107; Romans 7-8
18 Joshua 23-24; Psalm 108; Romans 9-10
19 Judges 1-2; Psalm 109; Romans 11-12
20 Judges 3-4; Psalm 110; Romans 13-14
21 Judges 5-6; Psalm 111; Romans 15-16
22 Judges 7-8; Psalm 112; 1 Corinthians 1-2
23 Judges 9; Psalm 113; 1 Corinthians 3-4
24 Judges 10-11; Psalm 114; 1 Corinthians 5-6
25 Judges 12-13; Psalm 115; 1 Corinthians 7
26 Judges 14-15; Psalm 116; 1 Corinthians 8-9
27 Judges 16-17; Psalm 117; 1 Corinthians 10
28 Judges 18-19; Psalm 118; 1 Corinthians 11
29 Judges 20-21; Psalm 119:1-88; 1 Corinthians 12
30 Ruth 1-4; Psalm 119:89-176; 1 Corinthians 13

MAY

1   1 Samuel 1-2; Psalm 120; 1 Corinthians 14
2   1 Samuel 3-4; Psalm 121; 1 Corinthians 15
3   1 Samuel 5-6; Psalm 122; 1 Corinthians 16
4   1 Samuel 7-8; Psalm 123; 2 Corinthians 1
5   1 Samuel 9-10; Psalm 124; 2 Corinthians 2-3
6   1 Samuel 11-12; Psalm 125; 2 Corinthians 4-5
7   1 Samuel 13-14; Psalm 126; 2 Corinthians 6-7
8   1 Samuel 15-16; Psalm 127; 2 Corinthians 8
9   1 Samuel 17; Psalm 128; 2 Corinthians 9-10
10 1 Samuel 18-19; Psalm 129; 2 Corinthians 11
11 1 Samuel 20-21; Psalm 130; 2 Corinthians 12
12 1 Samuel 22-23; Psalm 131; 2 Corinthians 13
13 1 Samuel 24-25; Psalm 132; Galatians 1-2
14 1 Samuel 26-27; Psalm 133; Galatians 3-4
15 1 Samuel 28-29; Psalm 134; Galatians 5-6
16 1 Samuel 30-31; Psalm 135; Ephesians 1-2
17 2 Samuel 1-2; Psalm 136; Ephesians 3-4
18 2 Samuel 3-4; Psalm 137; Ephesians 5-6
19 2 Samuel 5-6; Psalm 138; Philippians 1-2
20 2 Samuel 7-8; Psalm 139; Philippians 3-4
21 2 Samuel 9-10; Psalm 140; Colossians 1-2
22 2 Samuel 11-12; Psalm 141; Colossians 3-4
23 2 Samuel 13-14; Psalm 142; 1 Thessalonians 1-2
24 2 Samuel 15-16; Psalm 143; 1 Thessalonians 3-4
25 2 Samuel 17-18; Psalm 144; 1 Thessalonians 5
26 2 Samuel 19; Psalm 145; 2 Thessalonians 1-3
27 2 Samuel 20-21; Psalm 146; 1 Timothy 1-2
28 2 Samuel 22; Psalm 147; 1 Timothy 3-4
29 2 Samuel 23-24; Psalm 148; 1 Timothy 5-6
30 1 Kings 1; Psalm 149; 2 Timothy 1-2
31 1 Kings 2-3; Psalm 150; 2 Timothy 3-4

JUNE

1   1 Kings 4-5; Proverbs 1; Titus 1-3
2   1 Kings 6-7; Proverbs 2; Philemon
3   1 Kings 8; Proverbs 3; Hebrews 1-2
4   1 Kings 9-10; Proverbs 4; Hebrews 3-4
5   1 Kings 11-12; Proverbs 5; Hebrews 5-6
6   1 Kings 13-14; Proverbs 6; Hebrews 7-8
7   1 Kings 15-16; Proverbs 7; Hebrews 9-10
8   1 Kings 17-18; Proverbs 8; Hebrews 11
9   1 Kings 19-20; Proverbs 9; Hebrews 12
10 1 Kings 21-22; Proverbs 10; Hebrews 13
11 2 Kings 1-2; Proverbs 11; James 1
12 2 Kings 3-4; Proverbs 12; James 2-3
13 2 Kings 5-6; Proverbs 13; James 4-5
14 2 Kings 7-8; Proverbs 14; 1 Peter 1
15 2 Kings 9-10; Proverbs 15; 1 Peter 2-3
16 2 Kings 11-12; Proverbs 16; 1 Peter 4-5
17 2 Kings 13-14; Proverbs 17; 2 Peter 1-3
18 2 Kings 15-16; Proverbs 18; 1 John 1-2
19 2 Kings 17; Proverbs 19; 1 John 3-4
20 2 Kings 18-19; Proverbs 20; 1 John 5
21 2 Kings 20-21; Proverbs 21; 2 John
22 2 Kings 22-23; Proverbs 22; 3 John
23 2 Kings 24-25; Proverbs 23; Jude
24 1 Chronicles 1; Proverbs 24; Revelation 1-2
25 1 Chronicles 2-3; Proverbs 25; Revelation 3-5
26 1 Chronicles 4-5; Proverbs 26; Revelation 6-7
27 1 Chronicles 6-7; Proverbs 27; Revelation 8-10
28 1 Chronicles 8-9; Proverbs 28; Revelation 11-12
29 1 Chronicles 10-11; Proverbs 29; Revelation 13-14
30 1 Chronicles 12-13; Proverbs 30, Revelation 15-17

July

1   1 Chronicles 14-15; Proverbs 31; Revelation 18-19
2   1 Chronicles 16-17; Psalm 1; Revelation 20-22
3   1 Chronicles 18-19; Psalm 2; Matthew 1-2
4   1 Chronicles 20-21; Psalm 3; Matthew 3-4
5   1 Chronicles 22-23; Psalm 4; Matthew 5
6   1 Chronicles 24-25; Psalm 5; Matthew 6-7
7   1 Chronicles 26-27; Psalm 6; Matthew 8-9
8   1 Chronicles 28-29; Psalm 7; Matthew 10-11
9   2 Chronicles 1-2; Psalm 8; Matthew 12
10 2 Chronicles 3-4; Psalm 9; Matthew 13
11 2 Chronicles 5-6; Psalm 10; Matthew 14-15
12 2 Chronicles 7-8; Psalm 11; Matthew 16-17
13 2 Chronicles 9-10; Psalm 12; Matthew 18
14 2 Chronicles 11-12; Psalm 13; Matthew 19-20
15 2 Chronicles 13-14; Psalm 14; Matthew 21
16 2 Chronicles 15-16; Psalm 15; Matthew 22
17 2 Chronicles 17-18; Psalm 16; Matthew 23
18 2 Chronicles 19-20; Psalm 17; Matthew 24
19 2 Chronicles 21-22; Psalm 18; Matthew 25
20 2 Chronicles 23-24; Psalm 19; Matthew 26
21 2 Chronicles 25-26; Psalm 20; Matthew 27
22 2 Chronicles 27-28; Psalm 21; Matthew 28
23 2 Chronicles 29-30; Psalm 22; Mark 1
24 2 Chronicles 31-32; Psalm 23; Mark 2
25 2 Chronicles 33-34; Psalm 24; Mark 3
26 2 Chronicles 35-36; Psalm 25; Mark 4
27 Ezra 1-2; Psalm 26; Mark 5
28 Ezra 3-4; Psalm 27; Mark 6
29 Ezra 5-6; Psalm 28; Mark 7
30 Ezra 7-8; Psalm 29; Mark 8
31 Ezra 9-10; Psalm 30; Mark 9

August

1   Nehemiah 1-2; Psalm 31; Mark 10
2   Nehemiah 3-4; Psalm 32; Mark 11
3   Nehemiah 5-6; Psalm 33; Mark 12
4   Nehemiah 7; Psalm 34; Mark 13
5   Nehemiah 8-9; Psalm 35; Mark 14
6   Nehemiah 10-11; Psalm 36; Mark 15
7   Nehemiah 12-13; Psalm 37; Mark 16
8   Esther 1-2; Psalm 38; Luke 1
9   Esther 3-4; Psalm 39; Luke 2
10 Esther 5-6; Psalm 40; Luke 3
11 Esther 7-8; Psalm 41; Luke 4
12 Esther 9-10; Psalm 42; Luke 5
13 Job 1-2; Psalm 43; Luke 6
14 Job 3-4; Psalm 44; Luke 7
15 Job 5-6; Psalm 45; Luke 8
16 Job 7-8; Psalm 46; Luke 9
17 Job 9-10; Psalm 47; Luke 10
18 Job 11-12; Psalm 48; Luke 11
19 Job 13-14; Psalm 49; Luke 12
20 Job 15-16; Psalm 50; Luke 13
21 Job 17-18; Psalm 51; Luke 14
22 Job 19-20; Psalm 52; Luke 15
23 Job 21-22; Psalm 53; Luke 16
24 Job 23-25; Psalm 54; Luke 17
25 Job 26-28; Psalm 55; Luke 18
26 Job 29-30; Psalm 56; Luke 19
27 Job 31-32; Psalm 57; Luke 20
28 Job 33-34; Psalm 58; Luke 21
29 Job 35-36; Psalm 59; Luke 22
30 Job 37-38; Psalm 60; Luke 23
31 Job 39-40; Psalm 61; Luke 24

September

1 Job 41-42; Psalm 62; John 1
2 Ecclesiastes 1-2; Psalm 63; John 2-3
3 Ecclesiastes 3-4; Psalm 64; John 4
4 Ecclesiastes 5-6; Psalm 65; John 5
5 Ecclesiastes 7-8; Psalm 66; John 6
6 Ecclesiastes 9-10; Psalm 67; John 7
7 Ecclesiastes 11-12; Psalm 68; John 8
8 Song of Solomon 1-2; Psalm 69; John 9
9 Song of Solomon 3-4; Psalm 70; John 10
10 Song of Solomon 5-6; Psalm 71; John 11
11 Song of Solomon 7-8; Psalm 72; John 12
12 Isaiah 1-2; Psalm 73; John 13
13 Isaiah 3-5; Psalm 74; John 14-15
14 Isaiah 6-8; Psalm 75; John 16
15 Isaiah 9-10; Psalm 76; John 17
16 Isaiah 11-13; Psalm 77; John 18
17 Isaiah 14-15; Psalm 78; John 19
18 Isaiah 16-17; Psalm 79; John 20
19 Isaiah 18-19; Psalm 80; John 21
20 Isaiah 20-22; Psalm 81; Acts 1
21 Isaiah 23-24; Psalm 82; Acts 2
22 Isaiah 25-26; Psalm 83; Acts 3-4
23 Isaiah 27-28; Psalm 84; Acts 5-6
24 Isaiah 29-30; Psalm 85; Acts 7
25 Isaiah 31-32; Psalm 86; Acts 8
26 Isaiah 33-34; Psalm 87; Acts 9
27 Isaiah 35-36; Psalm 88; Acts 10
28 Isaiah 37-38; Psalm 89; Acts 11-12
29 Isaiah 39-40; Psalm 90; Acts 13
30 Isaiah 41-42; Psalm 91; Acts 14

OCTOBER

1 Isaiah 43-44; Psalm 92; Acts 15
2 Isaiah 45-46; Psalm 93; Acts 16
3 Isaiah 47-48; Psalm 94; Acts 17
4 Isaiah 49-50; Psalm 95; Acts 18
5 Isaiah 51-52; Psalm 96; Acts 19
6 Isaiah 53-54; Psalm 97; Acts 20
7 Isaiah 55-56; Psalm 98; Acts 21
8 Isaiah 57-58; Psalm 99; Acts 22
9 Isaiah 59-60; Psalm 100; Acts 23
10 Isaiah 61-62; Psalm 101; Acts 24-25
11 Isaiah 63-64; Psalm 102; Acts 26
12 Isaiah 65-66; Psalm 103; Acts 27
13 Jeremiah 1-2; Psalm 104; Acts 28
14 Jeremiah 3-4; Psalm 105; Romans 1-2
15 Jeremiah 5-6; Psalm 106; Romans 3-4
16 Jeremiah 7-8; Psalm 107; Romans 5-6
17 Jeremiah 9-10; Psalm 108; Romans 7-8
18 Jeremiah 11-12; Psalm 109; Romans 9-10
19 Jeremiah 13-14; Psalm 110; Romans 11-12
20 Jeremiah 15-16; Psalm 111; Romans 13-14
21 Jeremiah 17-18; Psalm 112; Romans 15-16
22 Jeremiah 19-20; Psalm 113; 1 Corinthians 1-2
23 Jeremiah 21-22; Psalm 114; 1 Corinthians 3-4
24 Jeremiah 23-24; Psalm 115; 1 Corinthians 5-6
25 Jeremiah 25-26; Psalm 116; 1 Corinthians 7
26 Jeremiah 27-28; Psalm 117; 1 Corinthians 8-9
27 Jeremiah 29-30; Psalm 118; 1 Corinthians 10
28 Jeremiah 31-32; Psalm 119:1-64; 1 Corinthians 11
29 Jeremiah 33-34; Psalm 119:65-120; 1 Corinthians 12
30 Jeremiah 35-36; Psalm 119:121-176; 1 Corinthians 13
31 Jeremiah 37-38; Psalm 120; 1 Corinthians 14

November

1 Jeremiah 39-40; Psalm 121; 1 Corinthians 15
2 Jeremiah 41-42; Psalm 122; 1 Corinthians 16
3 Jeremiah 43-44; Psalm 123; 2 Corinthians 1
4 Jeremiah 45-46; Psalm 124; 2 Corinthians 2-3
5 Jeremiah 47-48; Psalm 125; 2 Corinthians 4-5
6 Jeremiah 49-50; Psalm 126; 2 Corinthians 6-7
7 Jeremiah 51-52; Psalm 127; 2 Corinthians 8
8 Lamentations 1-2; Psalm 128; 2 Corinthians 9-10
9 Lamentations 3; Psalm 129; 2 Corinthians 11
10 Lamentations 4-5; Psalm 130; 2 Corinthians 12
11 Ezekiel 1-2; Psalm 131; 2 Corinthians 13
12 Ezekiel 3-4; Psalm 132; Galatians 1-2
13 Ezekiel 5-6; Psalm 133; Galatians 3-4
14 Ezekiel 7-8; Psalm 134; Galatians 5-6
15 Ezekiel 9-10; Psalm 135; Ephesians 1-2
16 Ezekiel 11-12; Psalm 136; Ephesians 3-4
17 Ezekiel 13-14; Psalm 137; Ephesians 5-6
18 Ezekiel 15-16; Psalm 138; Philippians 1-2
19 Ezekiel 17-18; Psalm 139; Philippians 3-4
20 Ezekiel 19-20; Psalm 140; Colossians 1-2
21 Ezekiel 21-22; Psalm 141; Colossians 3-4
22 Ezekiel 23-24; Psalm 142; 1 Thessalonians 1-2
23 Ezekiel 25-26; Psalm 143; 1 Thessalonians 3-4
24 Ezekiel 27-28; Psalm 144; 1 Thessalonians 5
25 Ezekiel 29-30; Psalm 145; 2 Thessalonians 1-3
26 Ezekiel 31-32; Psalm 146; 1 Timothy 1-2
27 Ezekiel 33-34; Psalm 147; 1 Timothy 3-4
28 Ezekiel 35-36; Psalm 148; 1 Timothy 5-6
29 Ezekiel 37-38; Psalm 149; 2 Timothy 1-2
30 Ezekiel 39-40; Psalm 150; 2 Timothy 3-4

One Year Bible Reading Plan

December

1   Ezekiel 41-42; Proverbs 1; Titus 1-3
2   Ezekiel 43-44; Proverbs 2; Philemon
3   Ezekiel 45-46; Proverbs 3; Hebrews 1-2
4   Ezekiel 47-48; Proverbs 4; Hebrews 3-4
5   Daniel 1-2; Proverbs 5; Hebrews 5-6
6   Daniel 3-4; Proverbs 6; Hebrews 7-8
7   Daniel 5-6; Proverbs 7; Hebrews 9-10
8   Daniel 7-8; Proverbs 8; Hebrews 11
9   Daniel 9-10; Proverbs 9; Hebrews 12
10 Daniel 11-12; Proverbs 10; Hebrews 13
11 Hosea 1-3; Proverbs 11; James 1-3
12 Hosea 4-6; Proverbs 12; James 4-5
13 Hosea 7-8; Proverbs 13; 1 Peter 1
14 Hosea 9-11; Proverbs 14; 1 Peter 2-3
15 Hosea 12-14; Proverbs 15; 1 Peter 4-5
16 Joel 1-3; Proverbs 16; 2 Peter 1-3
17 Amos 1-3; Proverbs 17; 1 John 1-2
18 Amos 4-6; Proverbs 18; 1 John 3-4
19 Amos 7-9; Proverbs 19; 1 John 5
20 Obadiah; Proverbs 20; 2 John
21 Jonah 1-4; Proverbs 21; 3 John
22 Micah 1-4; Proverbs 22; Jude
23 Micah 5-7; Proverbs 23; Revelation 1-2
24 Nahum 1-3; Proverbs 24; Revelation 3-5
25 Habakkuk 1-3; Proverbs 25; Revelation 6-7
26 Zephaniah 1-3; Proverbs 26; Revelation 8-10
27 Haggai 1-2; Proverbs 27; Revelation 11-12
28 Zechariah 1-4; Proverbs 28; Revelation 13-14
29 Zechariah 5-9; Proverbs 29; Revelation 15-17
30 Zechariah 10-14; Proverbs 30; Revelation 18-19
31 Malachi 1-4; Proverbs 31; Revelation 20-22